FROM *W*EEDS TO *W*ISDOM

Deborah Ruth Reaves

Library of Congress Control Number: 2022945363
                Paperback: 978-1958169-24-7
                eBook: 978-1-958169-13-1

Dedication

I dedicate this book to my husband, Alton, who has tirelessly given of his time, expertise, and material goods to make this book possible. How blessed I am to have such a loving and supportive husband! I also thank my God for two wonderful sons, Chuck, and Corey for their enduring love and for always being my great encouragers.

Acknowledgments

I would like to begin by acknowledging Jesus, who is my life. Without Him, I would have no reason to wake up. He has given me salvation and with that, purpose for life. He has continued to instruct my ears to hear, my eyes to see and my tongue to speak a word in due season. I pray that I will be found faithful when the Lord returns.

I cannot forget those who have believed in me and supported me throughout my life: My parents, Vernon, and Mabel Jones, who raised me according to my Godly bent; my wonderful siblings: Larry, Bobbie, Ronny, Joy, Jerry, and Juneil, and my six grandchildren.

Finally, I would like to highlight four special friends: Joan Griffin for her creative ideas and love; Denise Swain for her faithfulness and prayers; Karen Macaleer for her prayers and excitement about the original manuscript; and Norma Stephenson for her support and great graphic ideas.

Contents

May Jesus Christ be Praised!

Foreword

*F*rom *Weeds to Wisdom* was birthed as a means to endure excruciating therapy following a total knee replacement surgery. I had no idea that these writings would give way to a devotional book that would not only benefit me, but also many others.

For many years I asked God to make me more sensitive and open to His everyday presence around me. I began to see spiritual analogies for the things I observed in the natural. *Weed Lessons* was one of the first devotionals I wrote after noticing how weeds could miraculously endure through a season of extreme heat and drought. Although I thoroughly enjoyed writing each devotional, I enjoyed more the challenge of creating titles for them. I wanted these titles to become household words as others would read them.

Through my soul's eye, I envision life as a huge maze and God as being the God of "Nobody Knows What's Going to Happen." Daily, as I start out through my maze, the Holy Spirit and his word are my traveling companions as I face the various issues of life. For spending money, God presents me with a "Power Check" called Grace. This check never overdrafts and is always more than enough. Because the Holy Spirit is always with me and in me, all that I encounter becomes sacred. I must continuously ask myself this question: "How can I glorify God today?" Memorized scriptures surround me along the way. They teach me how to think about who and what I encounter so I can glorify God as I make my way to the finish line. This book is about some of the everyday things I have noticed in my daily maze and how God was glorified through them, again and again.

Scripture memorization has become of significant importance to me down through the years. But I must admit that I could never have imagined that God would eventually use an inanimate object, such as a clock to highlight one scripture in particular. Repeatedly, I would see the time 10:10 on different clocks. After this continued to happen, I began to think of scriptures that would fit "10:10" and it was then I remembered John 10:10: "For the enemy comes to kill, steal and destroy, but I have come to give you life, and give it to you more abundantly." I was amazed at how God would speak to me in such a unique way. Later, other scriptures began to make their regular appearances on different clocks as well. The numbers 8:18 reminded me of Romans 8:18 and 3:20 recalled both Revelation 3:20 and Ephesians 3:20. If I had not previously memorized these scriptures, the numbers on the clock would have been limited to just the time of day. Because of my scripture experiences with clocks, I felt compelled to include these and other scriptures in my Daily Power Maze as well as the Power Checks.

With *From Weeds to Wisdom*, it is my intention to motivate others to be poised to see and hear God in all of life and to encourage them to be thinking about Him every waking hour. I pray that God will richly bless you through the contents of this book.

An Ear to Hear

As the Lord has graciously permitted me to see a brand-new year,

He has caused me to ponder on what it means to have an ear to hear.

When seven different times He chose to emphasize this phrase,

It would behoove us to carefully listen up as we live in these final days.

What is He conveying to the church age of which I am a part?

To five of those churches, He admonishes them to be sure to guard their hearts.

I believe that the Laodicean church is the church age of today,

So, let's carefully examine what it is the Spirit has to say.

He begins by telling all of us that we are neither hot nor cold,

And we wrongly believe we're self-sufficient, while desperately needing

His "Gold."

It seems the modern-day church believes it has everything it needs,

While poverty, blindness, wretchedness, and nakedness are what it mainly breeds.

But for all of this wrong kind of thinking, Jesus has *the* remedy:

White clothes to wear for our nakedness and eye salve to help us see.

He makes it clear that the church believes it has no need for Him.

That's why He's now outside the door gently knocking to come in.

But this knock on the door is a special knock, not a knock for everyone's ears.

It's the kind of knock that can only be discerned by ears that have been trained to hear.

Jesus is trying to get our attention from the busy lives we lead.

He has stood so long knocking at that door as He continues to make His plea.

His invitation to open the door is extended to a select few:

To those who know His voice because abiding is what they do.

So, having an ear to hear what the Spirit has to say

Is so much more important than whatever we do today.

Be sill and know that God is God, tuning out all outward noise.

And inwardly you can connect with Him while quietly being poised.

It's time to stop whatever you're doing and listen for His voice,

So, you'll be among the selected few who'll fellowship with Him by choice.

"To Him who overcomes, I will give the right to sit with me on my throne, just as I overcame and sat down with my Father on His throne. He who has an ear to hear, let him hear what the Spirit says to the churches"

(Revelation 3: 21-22 NIV).

God be with you.

Deborah R. Reaves

Weed Lessons

"But blessed is the man who trusts in the Lord, whose confidence is in Him. He will be like a tree planted by the water that sends out its roots by the stream. It does not fear when heat comes; its leaves are always green. It has no worries in a year of drought and never fails to bear fruit"

(Jeremiah 17:7-8, NIV).

The summer of 1999 was a memorable one, at least for some parts of the east coast. It was a summer of absolute dryness, accompanied with extremely elevated temperatures and hideous brown lawns: a season of drought. Often, as I walked up the driveway from my car, I marveled at how both the grass and the weeds responded quite differently to the very same adversity. The only green things to be found on my lawn were the weeds. It was interesting to see that the weeds defied the adverse weather conditions and continued to thrive despite them. Daily, I found myself amazed at what I had observed, and it was as if God was drawing me to Himself, through these weeds, to teach me a new lesson.

I gradually began to see a wonderful spiritual parallel of this phenomenon: Even though we may suffer various trials in our lives, we can make the choice to defy them, to remain green, and to become even greener. Our adverse circumstances do not have to cause our demise. On the contrary, they can cause us to develop "long roots" that go down deep into the soil of our trials and produce life, not ordinary life, but life that is abundant and rich. Our hardships can work to aid us in developing "tough skin" for tough times!

I remembered that while the grass and flowers were delicate and would vanish away tomorrow, the weeds were divinely designed to be rugged, tenacious, enduring, and defiant. The weeds were actually glorifying the Creator as they refused to give in! Likewise, are we not called to be "heavy duty" in our Christian walk? Doesn't Paul encourage us to "run the race with perseverance" and not to "throw away our confidence or shrink back?"

What an encouraging lesson we can extract from such an insignificant and despised thing as a weed! Take heart saints, for it is never about the weather conditions, but all about the choice to glorify our God by fixing our eyes on Him as we stand in times like these.

Prayer: Heavenly Father, I marvel at how you reveal such deep spiritual truths to us through the ordinary things of life. Thank you for giving us eyes to see and hearts to learn from your creation. Give us daily strength and wisdom to become like the weeds, refusing to allow our adverse circumstances to dry us up. Instead, help us to be the only green things found on the landscape of your world. May we never faint or fear when the "drought" of our lives begins to set in. Amen.

Spandex Grace

"And God is able to make all grace abound to you, so that in all things at all times, having all that you need, you will abound in every good work"

(2 Corinthians 9:8 NIV).

Ilove to go shopping for clothes, but slacks are my least favorite item to buy. You see, with my full hips and thighs, I usually have difficulty finding slacks that will give me both a decent fit and will be comfortable all at the same time. Recently, I found a pair of slacks that I really liked; however, I was unable to try them on because there was no fitting room available. I decided to take a chance in purchasing them anyway. Before putting them on at home, I had already resigned myself to returning them because I was sure that they would not give me the good fit and the comfort that I desired. To my surprise, the slacks fit quite well, and it was only when I looked at the label that I understood why. Six percent of the fabric was made from spandex, a fabric that moves and breathes with one's body and provides a relaxed fit.

God's grace is like those spandex slacks. I think of it as *"Spandex Grace."* At this writing, I am undergoing very aggressive therapy for a recent total knee replacement surgery. There are two therapy treatments that I was required to do, and I often refer to them as the "Torture Chambers." When I was first introduced to the "Torture Chambers," I was required to endure them for 5 minutes. At that time, 5 minutes seemed like a lifetime because of the intense pain they caused. Initially, I "kicked and screamed" as one about to be put to the slaughter. Because I continued to struggle with 5 minutes of this torture, my heart nearly failed me when the therapist informed me that my time would be increased throughout the next several weeks. However, I am now capable of enduring 15 minutes of this same torture. Why? How? Well, it's God's incredible "spandex grace," grace that is capable of expanding to perfectly fit the very size and intensity of my specific need for a given time period, however long or short. Although God's "spandex grace" will never eliminate the pain and discomfort of the torture chambers, it is teaching me very great patience and endurance and to do what I must without whining or complaining. At times, I have even asked the therapist to increase the amount of weight on my knee so that I can hasten the recovery process. Not only am I able to survive those "Torture Chambers," but also, I am able to endure them with a quiet heart. God's grace really is sufficient! And we can count on Him to always be the head cheerleader in that great cloud of witnesses who so wonderfully encompasses us as we run the race of life!

Now I know that whenever I look at the "label of life," I will always find that the content of its fiber will most assuredly state: "100% Spandex Grace—One size Fits All." I also know that I can endure whatever trial or disappointment life brings because "spandex grace" will be there to accommodate me at every turn. I am learning that I will never again have to doubt the power of God's wonderful gift of grace because He gives us grace that is tailored for every single trial. There is absolutely no suffering that can out-do God's unique "Spandex Grace!"

Wow, "Spandex Grace!" It really is amazing! What would we ever do without it?

Prayer: Lord, your grace is really amazing! Thank you for making it expandable, capable of always fitting all things, and being more than enough. May you allow us many more challenging opportunities to experience you on higher levels, all because of your spandex grace. Amen.

PIP

"We demolish arguments and every pretension that sets itself up against the knowledge of God, and we take captive every thought to make it obedient to Christ"

(2 Corinthians 10:5 NIV).

Today we have so many gadgets that help to simplify our lives-or so we think! Take "PIP," translated: "Picture-in-a-Picture." This is a popular remote-control feature that enables one to view two different television channels simultaneously. "PIP" makes it possible to first see the larger picture on the original channel, and then, at the flick of a button, a smaller picture of an entirely different channel will appear within the larger one. You can even move the smaller image to the top right or left or bottom right or left of the larger picture. It's amazing! The whole idea of "PIP" is to make it possible for you to view two programs at the same time. However, the big problem with "PIP" is that you can never really see all either program because your mind is either partly on one or partly on the other. There is a dividing of the mind, and until you eliminate one, you will continue down the path of distraction.

In the spiritual realm, we often find ourselves in "PIP" situations. We press our "remote control" button to God's programming, only to find Satan continuously flicking in his "small picture" to distract us from what God wants us to see. We find ourselves struggling with the double mind syndrome as to whom we will obey. We have now entered a "PIP" scenario in which Satan takes great delight! Isn't this the very way he operated with Eve in the Garden of Eden? He distracted her from God's truth by presenting his innocent "small picture" of deception.

Because God knows we are totally incapable of dealing with a "PIP" environment in our own strength, He has provided for us a solution: To fix our eyes upon Jesus, the Author and Finisher of our faith. We are admonished to bring every thought into captivity to the obedience of Jesus Christ so that we can destroy every stronghold that imprisons us. At the simple flick of our "remote control unit," (a renewed mind which focuses on Christ and His word), we can eliminate every "SSPIGBP" ("Satan's Small Picture in God's Big Picture") and experience the victory we already have in Christ.

Prayer: Heavenly Father, I am grateful that you have provided a way of escape for every temptation we could face in this life. In our day-to-day living, we can so easily become distracted from your truth and struggle with what the enemy places before us on the "screens" of our minds. May we practice hiding your word in our hearts so that we can zap out the smaller picture that competes with your larger picture. May Christ be at the center of all our thoughts. Amen.

A Wardrobe Fit for A Saint

"Whose adorning let it not be that outward adorning of plaiting the hair, and of wearing of gold, or of putting of apparel; But let it be the hidden man of the heart"

(1 Peter 3:34a KJV).

"But put on the Lord Jesus Christ, and make not provision for the flesh, to fulfill the lust thereof

(Romans 13:14 NIV).

One of the great marks of a woman is that she is very conscientious about her appearance, whether it is her attire, hair, nails, or make-up. Annually, millions of women spend millions of dollars to look their best. Having the latest fashions, whether they are designer jeans, suits, or that special evening apparel, is high on the priority list of most women. Our closets are loaded with a variety of clothing styles to fit each occasion of life, but what about our spiritual wardrobe? Are we equally prepared to "dress" for the challenges we will encounter?

Our success in facing life's challenges will have a direct bearing on what we find hanging in our spiritual wardrobe. To be prepared, we must invest much of our time in abiding in the Lord, walking in intimacy with Him. It is only in intimate communion with Christ that we can acquire the garment of grace to endure; the garment of joy on which we focus while we press toward the mark; the garment of righteousness so that we can overcome Satan's lies; the garment of peace even in the midst of turmoil; the garment of the Word of God so that we can destroy every fiery dart of doubt, deceit, and denial shot at us by the enemy; the garment of compassion to minister to the brokenhearted; and, the garment of goodness to overcome evil. These are just some of the garments that make up a wardrobe fit for a saint. And just as we invest in physical clothing, we must invest in our spiritual attire as well. May we be diligent in acquiring the garments that count not only for the present time, but also for eternity.

Remember: In order to arise to every occasion life brings, we must have invested time abiding in the Lord, so that we can accumulate the Royal Garments we will need on that day! May we allow our rich Daddy (Abba) to lavish on us a complete makeover and a whole new wardrobe!

Prayer: Daddy, thank you for offering us a wardrobe fit for a saint. May you place in our hearts an unending desire to abide in you so that we can be dressed in Your best. Although you have given us all things to enjoy, and that includes the physical things, may we be more interested in what interests you, and that is our spiritual appearance. Let our spiritual closets be filled with the Royal Garments that will keep us prepared for the varied occasions of life. I love you, O Lord, my King. Amen.

Dead Men Can't Talk

"I am crucified with Christ: nevertheless, I live; yet not I, but Christ liveth in me; and the life which I now live in the flesh, I live by the faith of the Son of God, who loved me, and gave Himself for me"

(Galatians 2:20 NIV).

Before one dies, he may appoint someone to be the executor of his estate. The executor is someone in whom that person places his confidence, believing that all he has entrusted to him will be handled carefully and expeditiously. Upon death, the executor begins to act on behalf of the deceased and makes decisions accordingly. He now speaks for the deceased because the deceased can no longer speak for himself. Through death the deceased has abandoned his right to handle his own affairs, thus leaving the executor in the "driver's seat."

As I meditate on Galatians 2:20, this is the mental picture I see. When I first trusted Christ to be my personal Savior, I had essentially chosen Him to become "The Executor" of my life. I died to self and am no longer in charge of my affairs. I must remember that my Executor will now speak for me because dead men can't speak! Since placing my confidence in my Executor, I believe that He will never disappoint me in the handling of my affairs and will always have my best interest at heart.

Jesus Christ is "The Executor" of executors. And, since He is the only One who has perfectly lived out the Christian life, I know that I can confidently take my rightful place in the "back seat" and leave the driving to Him, after all He never lost a passenger, never lost His way, nor is He ever late. He knows the best route and He guarantees us a safe arrival to our destination every time. Jesus is not only the best Executor and Chauffeur, but He is also the world's greatest ventriloquist! He must be because dead men can't talk!

Prayer: Dear Heavenly Father, I want to thank you for drawing me to you through the sacrificial death of your Son. You have made Him my "Executor" and I know that I can live my life as one who is dead to self but alive to Christ. May you gently move me to the "back seat" when I forget that I am dead to self and cannot run my affairs. May I remember that Jesus is perfectly capable of speaking for me in every situation, and He is able to handle all my affairs in such a way that there will never be any disappointments. I love you, O lord, my Strength. Amen.

Benefits

"He that spared not His own Son, but delivered Him up for us all, how shall He not with Him also freely give us all things?"

(Romans 8:32, NIV).

Before I married my husband, the benefits from my teaching position were very insufficient, especially having been a divorced parent of two. I had to pay the full price for every prescription and that became quite expensive with the cost of pharmaceuticals being what they are. I also remember being told that my older son's oral surgery would be covered under my health insurance, only to learn that I would be responsible for both the doctor's bill and the hospital costs. I was always struggling to pay the medical expenses that accumulated because of illness or injury.

Marriage has changed my benefits problem dramatically! I have inherited an excellent dental and medical health insurance plan because of my changed relationship to the man who is now my husband.

Recently, I called to schedule a doctor's appointment as a new patient, and as I gave my health insurance credentials to the receptionist, I was immediately informed that my office visit would be covered. I was remembered how blessed I am to have such coverage with medical costs skyrocketing all the time.

When I "married" Jesus Christ, I inherited benefits that are "out of this world!" Although I must now see the doctor for my aches and pains, the time will come when this will not be necessary because I will receive an incorruptible body. The need for prescription plans will be come obsolete as will dental plans, and all provided by my heavenly Father through the shed blood of His Son. Life insurance will become a thing of the past because the day I received Christ as my personal savior, I became an heir of soul insurance!

How wonderful it is to know that that I can enjoy God's wonderful benefits both now and forevermore---all because of my relationship to Him!

Prayer: Father, you leave no stone unturned as you provide your children with all things richly to enjoy. The greatest of all the benefits we inherit from you is the gift of salvation, and your amazing "spandex grace" which wonderfully sustains us as we move heavenward. May we not only use your benefits, but also rejoice that you always make them available to us. We thank you that we are fully covered under your unique and wonderful benefits plan. Amen.

New Normals

'Moab has been at ease since his youth; he has also been undisturbed on his lees, neither has he been emptied from vessel to vessel, nor has he gone into exile. Therefore, he retains his flavor, and his aroma has not changed"

(Jeremiah 48:11 NIV).

.

Remember ye not the former things, neither consider the things of old. Behold, I will do a new thing"

What are "New Normals?" What do they look like? Well, "New Normals" are seasons of change in our lives that are normal for a given time. They manifest themselves in birth, youth, school, college, marriage, parenting, careers, health issues, etc.

I believe God uses "New Normals" in our lives to prevent us from becoming comfortable in our comfort zones. He introduces us to new roles and challenges that are designed for us to grow in His grace and depend totally on Him. For how else could we move from "New Normal" to "New Normal" apart from the wonderful grace of God?

There have been many "New Normals" in my life, including divorce, the empty nest, and retirement. However, in recent months my "New Normals" seem to be becoming increasingly challenging because they are occurring more often and involve both the physical and the emotional. I must admit that "New Normals" initially frighten me because I feel as if I am in a maze, not knowing from day to day, where to go or what to do. But I am learning that these "mazes" are really blessings in disguise because they are constantly reminding me that I must fix my eyes on Jesus and totally depend on Him to get me from this present "normal" to the next "New Normal."

Prayer: Lord, life is filled with one new experience after another. Although transitions are needful, they can be quite challenging. Being the creatures of habit as tend to be, it is so convenient to stay where we are: desiring the status quo if possible. Help us to see change as something that is good for us because it presents us with opportunities to move to a higher plane in our walk with you. May we not be frightened by the "New normals" in our lives but embrace them as steppingstones to spiritual development and maturity. May we feel encouraged that since you have safely and successfully navigated us through many previous changes, you will do nothing less as we experience the next ones. Thank you, Lord for your faithfulness even during life's "New Normals." Amen.

Focal Point

"Looking unto Jesus the Author and Finisher of our faith, who for the joy that was set before Him, endured the cross, despising the shame, and is set down at the right hand of the throne of God"

(Hebrews 12:2 NIV).

At this writing, I am undergoing aggressive therapy for a recent total knee replacement surgery. One of the exercises necessary for strengthening my knee is to stand on my operative leg, balancing myself on something called the dyno-disc. Since standing on the one leg on a flat surface is no easy task, you can imagine that the dyno-disc is even more of a challenge! In the process of doing these stands, I have learned that I can keep my balance for longer time durations if I focus on one specific thing. Therefore, when I set my eyes on one particular object, I can successfully balance myself on the dyno-disc for up to 55 seconds. Not only is visual focus important, but also mental focus. To succeed at this exercise, I must discipline myself to be mentally and visually focused, even if it means ignoring someone who wants to talk to me while I am doing the dyno-disc.

How true this is for our spiritual concentration. Focus is of utmost importance if we are to have a successful Christian walk. I am reminded of the scripture in Hebrews 12:2 which commands us to fix our eyes on Jesus, the Author and Finisher of our faith. But what is it about Jesus that we must make our focal point? Well, we are to imitate Jesus as He focused on the joy that was set before Him and not on the pain and shame of the cross. He focused on the resurrection rather than the crucifixion. He set His mind on His exaltation and not on His humiliation. His heart was set on pleasing the Father rather than pleasing Himself. Satan tried repeatedly to distract Him and to keep Him from accomplishing His Father's will, but Jesus, with a face like flint, stayed balanced on His "dyno-disc," and absolutely no one or nothing could make Him fall off! May we keep our eyes on the

One who can keep us from falling as we seek to do our heavenly Father's will.

Prayer: Lord, thank you for your example of focusing on the things that are eternal. May we learn from you what it means to have tunnel vision as we seek to please God. Equip us with everything good for doing your will, and may that equipment include focusing only on the joy that you have set before us. Amen.

From Set-ups to Bless-ups

"But as for you, ye thought evil against me; but God meant it unto good, to bring to pass as it is this day, to save much people alive"

(Genesis 50:20, KJV).

The scriptures are filled with saints who endured a lifetime of "set-ups." For example, the Acts church was set-up for sure defeat after Stephen was martyred. All hell broke loose, and all hope was suddenly gone. However, it was at this very time that God transformed Satan's set-up into a glorious "Bless-UP!" The persecution of the church resulted in the movement of the gospel into areas that would never have been reached otherwise.

One of the most long-suffering saints we read about in the scriptures was Joseph. Despite 13 years of being set-up by his brothers, Potiphar's wife, and forgotten by those who could have helped him, Joseph saw his set-ups as working out for his and his family's good. He experienced God transforming his Satan-created set-ups into God-created Bless-Ups as he rose to be second to Pharaoh, who was the most powerful man in the world at that time.

When we belong to Christ, we can expect a myriad of set-ups, all orchestrated by the enemy of our souls. However, if we remain strong and refuse to throw away our confidence, we can be certain that those set-ups will result in great "Bless-ups."

I believe that every set-up is an opportunity for the power of Christ to rest upon us, and when the power of Christ rests upon us, we can expect to become complete, mature, lacking in nothing. God is more concerned with how we respond to the set-up—our attitude---than He is with the results. The process is where long-suffering, peace, and patience are learned.

I am learning to take delight in set-ups because I know that God is up to something. I also know that although Satan and his associates think they are setting me up, they fail to see that God is actually setting them up to set me up so that He can bless me up. To God be the glory!

Prayer: Father God, there is absolutely no one who can handle a Satanic set-up like you. I love how you demonstrate your sovereignty when you overrule Satan's attempts to upset me. I stand amazed at how you have woven into your plan for my life, Satan's set-ups. You make a fool out of our enemy when you work everything, he does all together for the good for your children. The next time adversities hit, instead of complaining or giving way to panic, may we remember that our set-ups are being set-up for a Bless-Up! Thank you, Lord for giving us a new birth into a living hope. In Jesus' name, I pray. Amen.

Spiritual Ticker Tape

"Be careful to obey all the law my servant Moses gave you; Do not turn from it to the right or to the left, that you may be successful wherever you go. Do not let this Book of the Law depart from your mouth; meditate on it day and night, so that you may be careful to do everything written in it. Then you will be prosperous and successful"

(Joshua 1:79 NIV).

On the cable news channels it is common to see ticker tape news tidbits flashing across the lower part of the television screen. Ticker tape enables us to keep up with the latest news reports and updates. If you watch the news for a while, you will see the same news items being repeated all throughout the day. It acts as a visible informer and or reminder even though you are hearing the newscaster give an oral account of the latest developments. However, one day while I watched the news, I thought to myself: "Wouldn't it be great if God would "ticker tape" the screens of our souls with a reminder to always glorify Him in word and deed?"

Many times, we need to be reminded whom we serve and that everything we do must have pure motives and be done to glorify our Father alone. God's "Ticker Tape" messages would make a world of difference in how we spend our money; how we respond to the other driver; how we treat others who have hurt us; how we use our tongues; how we spend our time; making intimacy with the Lord a priority; how much time we spend reading our Bible.

We get so caught up in the world's ways and thoughts that we desperately need God's "Ticker Tape" flashing across the screens of our minds, 24/7/365. It is my desire that the Lord will "Ticker Tape" me daily so that I can work out my own salvation to the glory of God!

Prayer: Dear Lord, your saints need many reminders as we seek to walk with you. May you grant us the desire to draw nearer to you and abide in your word so that your "Ticker Tape" messages flash through our minds 24/ 7/ 365. Lord, if you would just "ticker tape" us with this reminder: "GLORIFY ME IN EVERYTHING YOU SAY AND DO TODAY," we would better live up to our purpose in life, and that is to please you. Help us to see and respond accordingly to your "Ticker Tape" day by day. In the name of

Jesus, I pray. Amen.

Invisible Tattoos

"Set me as a seal upon thine heart"

(Song of Solomon 8:6a KJV).

I am sure that you would agree with me that tattoos have become one of the biggest crazes of our times. They are in vogue for both the young and the not so young and worn in highly visible places all over the body. The latest tattoos are designed to make a statement. Unlike yesteryear, they are not only visible on arms, but also on ankles, feet, shoulders, necks, backs, breasts, and some rare cases, on faces. People are excited to be a part of the "in-crowd" as they flaunt their designer tattoos, and some consider their tattoo as a trademark or a special expression of their beliefs.

All this tattoo business motivated me to consider my own thoughts regarding them. It reminded me of Christians who have their own version of tattoos. Although their tattoos are not visibly seen on the flesh, they show up in works: saying the right things, doing virtuous deeds, and taking pride in their regular church attendance.

Tattoos were once indelible, permanently placed on the skin and applied with no small pain. But now, with advanced technology, I understand they can be removed through laser procedures. I must admit that the idea of tattoos is appealing to me, but only if they are invisible. Let me explain. I invite my heavenly Father to work in me both to will and to do of His good pleasure. In other words, I want Him to tattoo on my heart His love, compassion, gentleness, humility, kindness, patience, peace, and his rich word. Unlike the worldly visible tattoos, God's invisible tattoos are not just "talk," but they manifest themselves in a lifestyle. And not only are they invisible as well as visible, but also, they are placed as a seal on my heart by the hand of God and are good for eternity. God's invisible tattoos are not just the craze of the day, but they will speak much longer and louder than those skin tattoos ever could. They tell others that Christ is living in me. Now those are tattoos worth having!

Lord, place your tattoos all over my heart so that I can flaunt you everywhere! Glory to God!

Prayer: Dear Lord, may you be pleased to tattoo my heart with the qualities that will make me look more like you. May I be pleased to flaunt every tattoo you place on my heart so that everyone will say, "She looks like her Daddy!" Thank you for giving me tattoos that go beyond this life. Amen.

What God Taught Me in the Torture Chamber

"It is good for me that I have been afflicted, that I might learn thy statute"

(Psalm 119: 71 KJV).

The year of 2002 will go down in my personal history as one of the most physically challenging years of my life. It all started in January when I learned that it would be necessary for me to have a total knee replacement. The surgery occurred in March, and I really thought I had gotten through the worst of it, but little did I know that the "Torture Chamber" awaiteth me!

The "Torture Chamber," as I affectionately referred to it, was set up in the following manner: I was seated in a chair with my operative leg placed in another chair opposite me. The torture began when a roped pad was strapped around my operative knee. Next, the therapist, flexing his muscles, would pull up on the rope, forcing the knee to straighten out. The goal was to be able to extend my knee from −19 degrees to 0. I began spending 5 minutes in this contraption, but, eventually, I could tolerate 15 minutes. My "Torture Chamber" inauguration included being surrounded by the entire therapy staff as they presented me with a box of tissues for my tears. As the days became weeks, and the weeks became months, I began to realize that God had so much He wanted to teach me through this agonizing therapy treatment.

First, the Lord revealed to me that just as my knee was strapped to the roped pad, I was also strapped to my circumstances in life. You see I was not counting it all joy the cup God had assigned me. I even compared myself to others and wondered why their knee replacements did not require such aggressive therapy. I compared, complained, and wondered until I finally decided to accept my circumstances, good, bad, or ugly.

Secondly, patience and endurance became my friends as I learned that I couldn't rush God to heal my knee or to rush me through the difficult circumstances of life. God's timing guarantees perfectly ripe fruit and completeness.

Perseverance was another lesson learned in the "torture Chamber." Oftentimes, while looking at the timer and wondering if I could go the distance, my Lord would whisper, "You can do it! Keep your focus on me and I'll get you there!

I saw compassion while in the "Torture Chamber" when the therapist would periodically come by to check on me. He would often say, "Are you Okay, Deb?" Sometimes I would notice him watching me from a distance as though he could feel my pain. Other times when my timer was about to go off, he'd hover over me, ready to set my leg free.

I remember experiencing empathy when a former "Torture Chamber"

Victim got off the treadmill to give me a lifesaver. She had already been where I now was, and she knew all too well that, "A spoonful of sugar helps the medicine go down." The pain was so tremendous until I would eat candy, listen to Christian music on my walkman, sing, and do whatever else would temporarily distract me from this horrifying experience! However, after a few weeks, these distractions became ineffective, and it was then that I turned to writing. Writing in the "Torture Chamber" not only helped me to actively express the pain that I experienced, but it also made the time go by faster. God taught me to transform my pain into something positive and that has resulted in this and many other devotional writings that I hope to share with others who seek encouragement.

Although I have been in countless classrooms during my lifetime, not only as a student but also as a teacher, I have never experienced an education richer than that found in the classroom of God. No one can teach the lessons of life as Jesus can, but we must always come to Him with a teachable heart. On the first day of school, I would often tell my students that they would only get out of my class what they put into it. I would warn them that if they were to leave my class learning nothing and not becoming better for being with me, they would be at fault. I had already done my part to provide them a positive learning experience. In the same manner, God does His part in assigning us our lot. Now, we must emerge the better for having done something with it.

As I look back over this long and challenging year, I realize that 2 goals were achieved simultaneously. My knee has substantially improved, and I have learned to graciously accept my lot in life, whatever that may be. No time was wasted because I learned every single lesson that God wanted to teach me while in the "Torture Chamber." Would I do it all over again if required to do so? Absolutely! I wouldn't have missed the year 2002 for all the world!

Prayer: Lord, although it is so hard to endure the difficult circumstances of life, I want to thank you for extending your wonderful grace that has sustained me. I never would have experienced you in such spectacular ways had it not been for the "Torture Chamber." I now realize that these months of pain were not just about a knee that had to be replaced, but also more about the rich lessons of faith, patience, and grace that I would experience. Thank you, Lord for caring enough to teach me while in the "Torture Chamber." Amen.

Working with a Sword Handy!

"Those who carried material did their work with one hand and held a weapon in the other, and each of the builders wore his sword at his side as he worked."

(Nehemiah 4:17-18 NIV).

"Keep thy heart with all diligence; for out of it are the issues of life"

(Proverbs 4:23 KJV).

The book of Nehemiah has always fascinated me because of how Nehemiah dealt with his enemies. It seems that from the very beginning of the Jerusalem wall reconstruction, Sanballat and Tobiah were determined to undermine this God-ordained mission. They were relentless in their attempts to distract Nehemiah and his fellow workers from the job God had called them to do. The Bible first introduces us to these two evil men when it describes them as being "disturbed that Nehemiah had come to promote the welfare of the Israelites." Sanballat and Tobiah initially taunted Nehemiah with criticisms and then began to ridicule him regarding the re-building of the Jerusalem wall. When they realized that these tactics failed, their scheming activities escalated to various forms of intimidation, all to no avail. Nehemiah was so in tune with God that he was able to discern what was true or false. He prayed without ceasing and set up an organized plan of action to complete the task God had assigned him. Every man worked with a sword at his side, and some even strategically worked with one hand while holding a weapon with the other. A trumpeter was placed beside Nehemiah and was instructed to sound the trumpet when the enemy threatened trouble of any kind. Furthermore, none of the workers removed their clothing or their weapons at any time, and they planned for guard duty during the night hours.

I absolutely love this account of the wall reconstruction scenario because it is such a wonderful picture of how we must always guard our hearts. Recently, I was thinking of how difficult it is to guard my heart all through the day. It seems that as soon as I leave my prayer closet, the "Sanballat's" and "Tobiah's" of my life are waiting to attack me. Unfortunately, I have not always been prepared with an organized plan of action. Instead of being concerned about the relentless efforts of my "Sanballat's" and "Tobiah's," may I become relentless in standing against them by allowing the Christ in me to live through me with His sword at His side. May I resolve to never take off my Jesus Christ nor lay down my sword, which is His word. I pray that I would stay close to my Vine so that I may continually experience Holy Spirit wisdom, thus being able to discern the truth from a lie. During the night hours, my heavenly Father is pulling guard duty for me because He never slumbers or sleeps. He will preserve me from every form of evil, and will oversee my comings and goings, both now and always.

May God help us to follow Nehemiah's example by having a plan to guard our hearts with all diligence!

Prayer: Lord, it is so difficult to guard our hearts all through the day. As soon as we get off our knees, we are under attack, and so often losing the battle. May You start us off, reminding us that we are to take up Your armor and use it throughout the day as we go about the business of living. May we always be aware of our enemy and keep our swords handy as we work. Give us the attitude of Nehemiah who never let his guard down. Thank you, Lord. Amen.

Lord, Please Give Me A Bad Memory!

" And be ye kind one to another, tender hearted, forgiving one another, even as God for Christ's sake hath forgiven you"

(Ephesians 4:32 KJV).

Having a bad memory is becoming a conversation piece among the "Baby Boomers"! I know because I am a "Baby Boomer!" It is amazing how we can forget what we were planning to say right in the middle of a statement. And, how about when we get up to do something, we suddenly can't remember why we got up, let alone where we are going! Sometimes I must treat my memory with a little humor.

Although forgetfulness is a constant reminder of the aging process, I can see how it could be quite useful in the area of forgiveness. It wouldn't be a bad idea to pray that God would give us a bad memory when someone offends us. It is amazing how sharp our memory becomes when we suffer an insult, grief, or pain at the hand of another. We can give a detailed and clear account of everything that was said and done months and even years later. How nice it would be if we would remember to pray to forget. I remember a time when someone offended me by lying about me to someone else. Although I was deeply hurt, God enabled me to forget the incident in such a way that when the offender later apologized, I had to be reminded of what had happened. I would love to say that I always forget, but unfortunately, that was an exceptional case!

Our heavenly Father is such a wonderful example of forgiving and forgetting our sins all the time. It would be a good practice to pray that God will help us forget the transgressions of those who have offended us. The next time we are violated, let's remember to come down with a severe case of amnesia! Now that's a prayer request God would love to grant!

Prayer: Heavenly Father, help us to imitate you by releasing others who have hurt us. Work in us the will to forget those things that are so easy for us to remember. This can only be possible as we allow you to do through us what we cannot do ourselves. Remind us of our own shortcomings so that we can be more merciful to those who have offended us. In Jesus' name, I pray. Amen.

Right Under My Nose!

"According as His divine power has given unto us all things that pertain unto life and

Godliness" (2 Peter 1:3a KJV).

Today as I pulled out a pair of knee-high hose, I noticed that one was badly snagged. I had forgotten that the last time I wore them, my hands having been weather and water beaten, snagged every delicate thing I touched. I pondered over the many items I tried to help remedy my problem. I used everything from the over-the-counter lotions to the more expensive lotions and oils, all of which did not fix my hands. Latex gloves were the only thing that prevented me from snagging my hose until I stumbled over something that was amazingly helpful---good old water! I found that water-soaked hands make it a cinch to put on my hose without snagging them. I was pleasantly surprised to discover this and no longer had to be concerned about whether the lotions or oils would help. The solution was right under my nose!

We tend to do the same thing with God. When we are looking for solutions to our problems whether they are marriage, child rearing, finances, or life decisions, we often turn to the world's ways of doing things. We manage, exploit, manipulate, and try to control until we see the things around us starting to fold, and it is then and only then we realize that God, our "Way-Maker," was right under our nose all the time.

Be cautious not to waste time or money searching for solutions that do not work. Instead, may God be your first resort rather than your last. Just as something so simple as water can solve my "snagging" problem, so can God solve my life problems.

Prayer: Lord, you are so good at teaching your spiritual truths through the everyday things of life. May we be diligent in running to you at the very beginning of a problem, for you know every answer to every question, even ones such as how to prevent snags in my hose. Thank you for giving us everything we need to live and be godly. Amen.

Flood Proof Toilets

"And He said unto me, 'My grace is sufficient for thee; for my strength is made perfect in weakness.' Most gladly will I rather glory in my infirmities that the power of Christ may rest upon me"

(2 Corinthians 12:9 KJV).

When my husband and I moved into our new house, it was not long before we learned something about our toilets. Occasionally, one of the toilets would become backed up and when we attempted to flush it, the water would begin to rise to the top only to suddenly stop. Having had toilets overflow on us in the past, we were quite pleased to find that these newer toilets were designed to prevent overflowing problems. Although the water would rise to the very top, it always stopped just in the "nick of time!"

Sometimes our circumstances can be like those toilets: Flood proof! Just when we reach our breaking point, *Grace* happens. I remember the first week of physical therapy for my total knee replacement rehabilitation. Each therapy session involved the bending and straightening of my knee as well as measurements being taken to determine how many degrees I had to go to reach my goal. I became so frustrated and stressed out from all those painful measurements and exercises that I cried out to the Lord, "I am tired of all of this! I have had enough of the therapists measuring my knee and constantly discussing the number of degrees it would take to accomplish my goal!" I had reached my point of overflowing, but just as the toilet shut down to prevent its overflowing, I, too, experienced the same thing when I returned to therapy the next week. God had wonderfully enabled me to stop short of overflowing as He renewed my inward man. He made it possible for me to complete a rigorous course of therapy over a 5-month period so that I could successfully reach my goal. I praise God for "flood proof" Holy Spirit Power!

Prayer: Thank you Father for your wonderful and all sufficient grace. I am learning that it is only when I come to the end of myself that You are ready and waiting to step in and grant me a fresh supply of your grace. The longer I live, the more I can see that Your grace was designed to enable me to face life's unforeseen hardships and difficulties with confidence and perfect peace. Thank you, Daddy that Your power is available to rest on me when I am too weak to go on. In Jesus' name, I pray. Amen.

Mouth-to-Mouth Resuscitation

"The Lord put a message in Balaam's mouth and said, 'Go back to Balak and give him this message.'"

(Numbers 23:5 NIV).

"He answered, 'Must I not speak what the Lord puts in my mouth?'"

(Numbers 23:12 NIV).

Recently, during my quiet time with the Lord, I came across several scriptures that specifically refer to the mouth. For the past year, I have been asking the Lord to "tame my tongue" and to help me to speak only what He places in my mouth. As I meditated on these scriptures, I was reminded of mouth-to-mouth resuscitation. Several years ago, during my teaching career, our faculty and staff were in-serviced in CPR. I watched as the instructor positioned the dummy, tilted its head back, and then checked the mouth and throat for any obstructions. Finally, he opened the dummy's mouth and began to administer mouth-to-mouth resuscitation.

Isn't that like what God did to Balaam, Isaiah, Ezekiel, Jeremiah, and the psalmists? He administered spiritual mouth-to-mouth resuscitation. In each case, God placed His life-changing words in the mouths of His servants.

Just as CPR revives an unconscious person, so it is with one in whom God has placed His words. Not only is the speaker revived, but also those to whom the speaker speaks. As I reflect on the Biblical CPR accounts, I see that God's word was multi-purposeful: Balaam blessed rather than cursed the Israelites; Isaiah was given the word to sustain the weary; God placed His words in the mouths of Ezekiel and Jeremiah in order to admonish His people; the psalmist received a new song in his mouth—a song of praise to God.

I have decided that I need and desire God's version of mouth-to-mouth resuscitation. You see, my tongue needs to be tamed, and I do not always use my words with restraint. I stand in desperate need of a mouth revival and Jesus is the only one who can pull this off! So now, I start off my day requesting God's mouth-to-mouth resuscitation. May I say as did Balaam, "Must I not take heed to speak only what God has placed in my mouth?" With that kind of spiritual CPR, may I find it easier to face God and myself at the end of each day!

Prayer: Lord, I do desire the same kind of mouth-to-mouth resuscitation you administered to Balaam, the prophets, and the psalmists. I cannot speak what you would have me speak without your divine intervention. May the words of my mouth bless, encourage, and lovingly admonish others, while at the same time, praise you. Thank you, lord, for providing me with beauty tips for my tongue. May you be glorified! In the powerful name of Jesus, I pray. Amen.

But....

"But all this gives me no satisfaction as long as I see that Jew Mordecai sitting at the king's gate"

(Esther 5:13 NIV).

Recently, I have been studying the book of Esther with a Bible study group. The format of this study includes the highlighting of each major character in the book of Esther. During my study of Haman, I noticed something that convicted me about myself. Haman was the real villain of Esther as he became obsessed with Mordecai's refusal to bow down to him. The Bible states:

> "Haman went out on that day happy and in high spirits. But when he saw Mordecai at the king's gate and observed that he neither rose nor showed fear in his presence, he was filled with rage against Mordecai. Nevertheless, Haman restrained himself and went home.
>
> Calling together his friends and Zeresh, his wife, Haman boasted to them about his vast wealth, his many sons, and all the ways the king had honored him above the other nobles and officials. "And that's not all," Haman added. "I'm the only person Queen Esther invited to accompany the king to the banquet she gave. And she has invited me along with the king tomorrow. But all this gives me no satisfaction as long as I see that Jew Mordecai sitting at the king's gate'
>
> (Esther 5:9-1 NIV).

That "But" is where I see myself! You see, sometimes I am so busy majoring on the minors that I forget the many majors in my life. I can have one hundred blessings going for me on the one hand, and one minor setback on the other hand, and guess which one I accentuate? One such detail can make the difference between enjoying life and being miserable. The "minors" may be a negative comment during many positive ones. It can be a situation in which I noticed that a person did not attend one of my social affairs, although it was well attended by so many others. There's always that "But" that can take me for a loop! Unlike Haman, I do have the Lord to guide me back to all truth. He gives me a badly needed "spiritual slap" through the counsel of others or He just plain convicts me of the "But's" in my life as He highlights all the blessings.

Haman's attitude towards Mordecai resulted in his own demise, as the very gallows that he built for Mordecai would eventually become his very own destiny!

It is my desire to accentuate the "majors" and leave the "minors" to God because the "minors" can lead to a major downfall!

Prayer: Dear Lord, how shameful I feel when I overlook all your wonderful blessings and complain about the insignificant things in life. Please remind me when I do this and teach me to major on what really is important. May I learn to leave the "But's" in life out of my life. Thank you, lord for showing me my self through the attitude of Haman and thank you for loving me too much to leave me where I am. Amen.

Defeated Doesn't Live Here Anymore!

"Do not lie to each other, since you have taken off your old self with its practices and have put on the new self, which is being renewed in knowledge in the image of its Creator"

(Colossians 3:9-10 NIV).

It all started one Sunday afternoon while I was having my quiet time with the Lord. My husband had just left to go to a meeting when I began to hear a repetitive noise downstairs. The noise sounded like the opening and closing of our garage doors. At first, I thought my husband had returned from his meeting early, so I ignored this noise. Finally, when I did decide to go downstairs to investigate, I discovered that one of our garage doors would repeatedly go up and down. Although I saw this happening with my own eyes, I could not understand its cause. When my husband returned home, after sharing this with him, he explained to me that our garage door remote control unit was on the same frequency as that of our neighbors. When they would open and close their garage doors, ours would respond to their signal because they happen to be on the same frequency! My husband repaired the problem by changing the frequency on our remote-control unit, and this simple change allowed our garage door to respond to a different command.

This entire ordeal reminded me of how the enemy operates in the lives of the saints. He owns and operates 2 remote control units, after all, control and glory are his chief objectives. He uses the first remote control unit to turn on a hopeless scenario on the "Big Screen" of our souls. Satan loves to appeal to our sight, but he knows he must use the second remote control unit to get a "rise" out of us regarding that scenario on the "Big Screen." Unfortunately, this is where we faint, quit, give up, and throw away our confidence. We panic at what we see! However, we must remember our identity in Christ and what it looks like. We must remember that because we are no longer on Satan's frequency, we should no longer respond to his commands. In other words, "Defeated doesn't live here anymore" because Jesus changed our frequency at Calvary so that only in Him, we live, move, and have our very being!

Prayer: Heavenly Father, thank you so much for rescuing me from the dominion of darkness into the Kingdom of Light where your Son is. It is so reassuring to know that I am no longer on the enemy's frequency. Please help me to be more than a conqueror by responding to what I know about you. I love you O Lord, my Strength. Amen.

Soul Visions

"For physical training is of some value, but godliness has value for all things,

holding promise for both the present life and the life to come"

(1 Timothy 4:8 NIV).

Immediately following my many months of physical therapy, I enrolled in a fitness center. As I frequently traveled pass this facility, I often wondered about its name: "Body Visions." It was during my first visit, when I requested a personal trainer, that I began to understand the idea behind the name. In my initial interview, the trainer asked me what changes I would like to see in my body; what were my goals and what parts of my body did I want to work on. I like the thought of beginning my training with a vision—a customized plan---for what I personally desired for the development of my physical body.

Pondering about "Body Visions," I thought: "This whole concept would be a great approach to my soul's total development." I further reflected on my soul's need for a vision—a goal for growth and development, and I remembered that just a few short years ago, I had begun the process of planning a soul fitness program. You know how we tend to make New Year's resolutions for ourselves regarding weight loss and becoming more physically fit? Well, I decided that I wanted something more substantial and eternal for my soul since my body was only temporal. At the end of the year 2000, I began to seek God's direction for what I should ask Him to work in me for 2001. Although I had never thought of it in this way until now, I had already begun a soul fitness plan for myself. I had been actively setting goals for my soul.

Just as having a vision for my total physical development will help me to reach my bodily goals, so much more will having a soul visions plan, prescribed for me by my heavenly Trainer, guarantee that I will successfully reach the goal.

Prayer: Lord, there is so much we can learn about spiritual things from the physical. Although it is important to take care of my body because it is the temple of God, it is much more important to you that I be concerned with how I am doing spiritually. Thank you for working in me both to will and do of your good pleasure, as you motivate me to set goals for my soul. It is such a good thing to always keep before me "Soul visions!" In the name of Jesus, I pray. Amen.

Breast Feeding

"Then Peter, turning about, seeth the disciple whom Jesus loved following, which also

leaned on His breast at supper, and said, Lord, which is he that betrayeth thee"

(John 21:20 KJV).

I love to see a baby being nursed by his mother. In the church I attend, there is a considerable number of young women who are in the childbearing and breast-feeding season of life. During our weekly Bible study meetings, it is common for these mothers to retrieve their babies from the nursery to breast feed them. I have noticed that the babies seem peaceful, content, and completely satisfied as they nurse from their mother's breast. What a beautiful picture of spiritual "Breast Feeding."

In the book of John, we read several scriptures where John, the beloved disciple, describes himself as the one who lovingly leaned on the breast of Jesus, the Christ. I decided that I would like this to be the way of life for me. Rather than leaning on my own understanding, I desire to lean on the Lord for my daily breast feedings of His word. Just as a baby is content during his breast feedings, likewise, I can find contentment as the Lord feeds me with the "milk" of His word. Although all hell may be breaking loose in the world, I can breast feed peacefully and be fully satisfied because of all the good nourishment I am getting from God's word and just resting in His presence. Spiritual breast-feeding is a wonderful way to learn of Him while taking on His yoke, but we must be close to Him so that we can be in position to lean. Rather than depending on ourselves for direction and purpose in life, may we lean back, as did John, on the breast of the One who knows the way-- all because He is the Way. I want to be a "Johnetta" ---one who leans on the breast of my Lord so that I will know the heart of Him who loves me and cares for me. Spiritual "Breast Feedings" are the only means to face the challenges we encounter in life. They can allow people to see that we have such intimacy with Jesus that they will ask us to speak to Jesus on their behalf, just as Peter requested of John. John was always close enough to Jesus to know His heart. May we daily crave pure spiritual milk that can only come from leaning on the breast of our Savior!

Prayer: Lord, God, I do want to hear your marching orders for my life and get to know you at deeper levels. Daily, may I draw nearer to you so that you can count me worthy of your calling, and by your power, fulfill every good purpose of mine and every act prompted by my faith. "Breast feed" me, Lord, so that your heart will become mine. Amen.

As Quiet as Snow

"Then a voice said to him, 'What are you doing here, Elijah?' He replied, 'The Israelites have rejected your covenant, broken down your altars, and put your prophets to death with the sword. I am the only one left, and now they are trying to kill me too.' The Lord said to him, 'Yet I reserve seven thousand in Israel—all whose knees have not bowed down to Baal and all whose mouths have not kissed him.'"

(1 Kings 19: 13-14; 18 NIV).

The winter of 2003 will go down in history as one of the most unforgettable winters in the Northeastern part of the United States. We were bombarded with 23 inches of snow that shut down most businesses and left many homebound for a few days! It amazes me that all that snow could accumulate in such a brief time and in such a quiet manner. Snow tends to begin and end so quietly that if it falls during the night hours, you will never suspect that it was happening. There have been many times when I have awakened to find that throughout the night snow had fallen, and I never heard it.

God is like snow! He may move in a quietness that we may never see coming our way. How often we pray for God to change our circumstances or grow us up in our salvation. We pray about God delivering our loved ones from a particular sin, or to save another. We become frustrated, as we see no change. There is no evidence of the snow. However, while we are "sleeping," the "snow falls quietly" and we awaken to find that God has been there. We see evidence that God was working so quietly that we were completely unaware that He had heard us.

Many times in my life, I have experienced that God's blessings, just like the snowstorms of 2003, have "accumulated" on me. We often complain of the opposite: "When it rains, it pours!" But how wonderful it is when we find that God has quietly "snowed" in our lives, and at times with such abundance. All along He was quietly working things out for good, and at the same time, letting us know that He was acknowledging us—mere mortals. Although we may not always hear Him, we awaken and see that his divine intervention has quietly fallen on our lives and on those for whom we make intercession. Thank you, Lord for your faithfulness, even when it comes without sight or sound!

As a postscript to this devotional, God quietly "snowed" His blessings on me when this manuscript was accepted for publishing. I was completely surprised to find that God, once again, was quietly working while I was not looking.

Prayer: Dear Lord, I want to thank you for your faithfulness that extends to the heavens. Even when I don't see any evidence that you have heard my prayer, I later learn that you were there all the time, working out every detail to your glory. Thank you for your "quiet work" because it encourages me more to walk by faith and not by sight. God forbid that we should throw away our confidence when we do not see immediate answers to our prayers. May we hang in there with you until we "wake up" and find that snow has fallen while we slept. Thank you, my Lord. Amen.

Visitation Rights

"I am the Vine; you are the branches. If a man remains in me and I am him, he will bear much fruit; apart from me, you can do nothing"

(John 15:5 NIV).

We hear so much about visitation rights today with the divorce rate steadily skyrocketing. Often, children being used as pawns are denied visitation rights. They are denied the right to fellowship with the absent parent and as a result, the suffering is great.

When we grieve or quench the Holy Spirit, we are also denying ourselves visitation rights with our heavenly Father. Every time we ignore the Holy Spirit's leading in our lives, we quench Him and when we quench Him, we prevent ourselves from fellowshipping with our Father, God.

Another way in which we prevent "Visitation rights" between God and ourselves, is failing to abide in our Vine, Jesus Christ. When we live our life apart from God's leading and say in essence, "I can do it all by myself," we are denying the desperately needed "visitation rights" between ourselves and the members of the Trinity, as they attempt to work in and for us. How sad it is to see a parent deny visitation rights between the child and the absent parent; However, how much more devastating it is to see a redeemed soul fainting all because it has been denied "Visitation Rights" with God, the Father. We must protect our quiet times with the Lord because those regular visits with Him are where we receive His marching orders, His wisdom, His strength, and His discernment for our daily living. Let's stay connected!

Prayer: Lord, please forgive me for all the times I missed out on my "Visitation Rights" with you because I allowed other things to distract me. I desperately need these visits with you, or how else could I live my life according to your perfect plan? Absolutely nothing can satisfy the deep longings of my heart the way you do.

I need you, Lord, and it is my desire to spend more time being taught by you. Thank you for your transforming power that can only occur when I act on my "Visitation Rights." In the powerful name of Jesus, I pray. Amen.

From Water to Wine

"And the master of the banquet tasted the water that had been turned to wine. He did not realize where it had come from, though the servants who had drawn the water knew"

(John 2:9 NIV).

In the second chapter of John's gospel, we are blessed to see Jesus' involvements in the everyday things of life, such as a wedding. But this chapter reveals much greater things than Jesus' attendance at this particular wedding. It was because of His presence that the miracle of the wine and water occurred. We can learn so much about water than we realize. After Jesus learned that the wine had run out, He ordered the servants to fill the jars with water and it was only after this was done, that He performed His first miracle. The servants discovered that Jesus had changed the water into wine *only* when they began to dip it up to be served! Everyone was amazed to find that this was the best wine served at the wedding.

As I studied this passage, I marveled at the wonderful spiritual truths the Holy Spirit revealed to me. First, for Jesus to perform this miracle, it would be necessary for the servants to do their part: fill the jars with water. I call this the "water" part. This is the part we do—this is what we bring to Jesus, and God makes even that part possible. Next, Jesus took the "water" part and changed it into wine, not ordinary wine, but the best wine. That's the "God" part. Thirdly, the servants were instructed to serve the wine, and it was when they served it that they discovered it had been changed. The master of the banquet told the bridegroom that the best wine had been saved for last. No one knew the origin of this wine except those who were privy to what had happened.

Now, let's apply these spiritual truths to our everyday situations in today's times. Jesus is still in the "water-changing" business if we obey His instructions to us. For example, when we use our gifts to minister to the body of Christ, our first instruction is to commit these gifts to the Lord and use them only in the strength of His power. When we do this, we will find that miracles do occur---our "water" becomes "wine" as the Lord works through us to touch others. May we remember that apart from Jesus, we are nothing; neither can we do a thing. Therefore, it is my prayer that we allow Jesus to do miracles through us today as He transforms our ministry "from water to wine!"

Prayer: Heavenly Father, you are everything to me. You are a "Way-Maker" as well as a "Wine-Maker." I want to thank you that ministry gifts can never be effective without you being included in the equation. Thank you for making it clear in this story of the "The Wedding of Cana," that you do all things well when we first obey your instructions. I pray that we will always remember to strip ourselves of ourselves and present what's left for you to fill. Lord, I know that then and only then, will you be pleased to change us "from water to wine." Thank you, Lord. Amen.

Soulscaping

"Though you have not seen Him, you love Him; And even though you do not see Him now, you believe in Him and are filled with an inexpressible and glorious joy, for you are receiving the goal of your faith, the salvation of your souls"

(1 Peter 1:8-9 NIV).

Spring is my favorite time of the year for so many reasons: new buds appear, giving way to an assortment of colors that only God can create. Birds are cheerfully singing in the start of each new day while our heavenly Father is miraculously rejuvenating the landscape. In other words, everything comes alive and starts to grow.

This past spring, I decided to have some elaborate landscaping done on my front lawn, being that I could no longer do the work myself. This was neither a small nor inexpensive task. But when the work was completed, there appeared to be so little to show for all the labor and expense. I almost felt disappointed because what I had imagined for the results just did not seem to materialize. Having prayed diligently about my decision to get this landscaping done, I had to listen to what God was saying about all of this.

My heavenly Father invested His only begotten Son to bring me to a place of salvation. With great expense and labor, Jesus took on the task of soulscaping me. He transformed my soul to something new when He removed all the "weeds" from my life. He transplanted His heart to mine and began the process of planting the fruit of the Spirit within me. At first, as with my landscaping, it seemed a very futile effort. The plants were so tiny with little foliage or fruit. But the Lord began to show me that the newly landscaped lawn was a physical picture of my newly soulscaped soul. Fruit bearing is a process and will require much time, patience, and care before the good appears. I was given instructions to daily water my plants the first week and then twice weekly for one year. In the spiritual realm, God carefully instructs us to abide in Him for He is our Vine---our life support---the source of our fruit bearing. In both the physical, (Landscaping), and the spiritual, (Soulscaping), we must depend on the Lord to bring the increase, but we must be positioned where He can complete the process. I look forward to when the fruit of all the labor and expense invested in my lawn, will become visible. But more importantly, I look forward to the time when the fruit of my faith, begun by my heavenly Father, will be realized, full bloom in eternity with Him.

Prayer: Dear Lord, you always know what you are doing and what the plan is for our lives. Your timing and the faith and patience you invest in us work together to give us more than we expected. Although we may not yet see fully developed fruit in our lives, by faith we know that one day all the expense and labor you invested in us will give way to the most beautiful flower garden ever. Thank you, Lord. Amen.

"Got Junk?"

"For it was for freedom that Christ has set us free"

(Galatians 5:1 NIV).

A few months ago, someone left a flyer on our door that stated, "Got Junk?" It was an advertisement to have any junk removed from your home and hauled off. I became interested because I could think of several items I owned that had become useless to me. With some of them being quite heavy and bulky, this advertisement sounded very appealing. Ironically, to my surprise, God decided to apply the words of this flyer to my spiritual needs.

For the past several years, I had been accumulating quite a bit of clutter in my soul. Worries, fears, disappointments, health issues, anger, resentment, bitterness, hopelessness, frustrations, shame, and despair along with a host of other things, had made a resting place of my soul. I desperately needed to be uncluttered because, believe me, I had a lot of junk. During the Spring of 2004, God decided that it was high time for a thorough Spring cleaning. With a kind of urgency, I found myself un-cluttering the storage areas under the bathroom sinks. I even invested in storage bins so that there would be some rhyme and reason to the items stored there. I discarded much of the junk until everything was decent and in perfect order. Next, I began the tedious process of removing and bagging up clothing and shoes to give away to charity. Prior to this, our once barren and messy basement had been transformed into a place of beauty. Even our yard received a desperately needed makeover, and several shrubs were removed. When all this un-cluttering was completed, I wondered why I had been driven to do this. The answer came from God's still small voice when He said: "Just the way you un-cluttered your bathroom vanities, I am going to un-clutter your soul. Remember how barren, dark, and un-inviting your basement used to be? It now has a warm ambience and has become a place of beauty and calm. Likewise, I will transform you soul into a place of beauty." And so, just as God said, He began the process of de-cluttering me. Much of the "junk" that I had stored up in me has now been removed. I am beginning to feel whole, not half. I feel free, not inhibited. I feel like I am soaring, not bound to a weight of issues. With confidence, I can now enter into my divine calling, for God has removed from me and hauled away the junk in my soul. What about you? Got junk? Let Jesus take you on one of His Spring-Cleaning sprees and you will begin to experience the Abundant Life He came to give us.

Prayer: Dear Lord, help me to stay close to you so I can hear you reminding when my soul needs to be de-cluttered. Life moves along so swiftly, and I hardly notice all the baggage that so quickly accumulates. Please continue to de-clutter my mind and soul so that I can live out the abundant life you came to give me. Amen.

Seeing in Spiritual 3-D

"But God has revealed it to us by His Spirit. The Spirit searches all things, even the deep things of God'

(1 Corinthians 2: 10 NIV).

Several years ago, I visited my friend, Karen in Florida for a few days. While there, we decided to go to the Universal Studios in Orlando for a day outing. What fun it was to learn about the making of many familiar television shows and movies! One of the highlights of our Universal trip was "The Terminator." At the entrance, we were instructed to grab a pair of 3-Dimensional glasses for use during the presentation. I remember how vastly different things appeared when I viewed the screen with these special glasses. I could see birds, bats, and various other flying objects coming out of the screen towards me. But when I took off the glasses, my vision was limited only to what was on the screen. The movie would have been uneventful and ordinary had I not seen it from the 3-D perspective.

I believe a woman after God's own heart has spiritual 3-D vision. She does not stop at seeing the surface things of God, but she has a heart to go deeper. She is never satisfied with the status quo but desires the deep things of God: Things that no eye has seen, no ear has heard, no mind has conceived. No other in the scriptures has ever been referred to as "A man after God's own heart" except David. As I thought about a woman after God's own heart, I went back to David to see why he had been described as such. The answer is found in 1 Samuel 13:13-14. God was looking for a man who would completely obey His commands, and Saul was not that man, for he fell into a pattern of half-obeying God while believing that he was doing all that God desired. It was here Samuel announced that God would be placing on the throne a leader who would seek after His heart.

A woman after God's own heart is a woman who is willing to obey God completely—a woman who constantly does what is right (Psalm 106:3). She is a woman like Abigail, who daily walks in the wisdom of the Lord as she waits for a breakthrough. She chooses the better part when she allows Jesus to set the tone for her entire day. She acknowledges the Lord for direction in every choice and decision, no matter how major or minor. In other words, a woman after God's own heart is poised to see all of life from her Lord's perspective because abiding in Him is her way of life. Just as with the 3-D glasses, the eyes of her heart can see so much more of God, and she is prepared to be completely obedient to that vision.

Prayer: Lord, it is my desire for you to give me your 3-D vision so that I can become a woman who is sold out for you. Draw me closer to you and take me to a higher level of seeing and being. I know that one of the main ingredients for being a woman after your own heart is complete obedience and so I ask you to strengthen me in this area. Amen

High-Definition Pottery

"For I know the plans I have for you," declares the Lord, "Plans to prosper you and not to harm you, plans to give You hope and a future."

(Jeremiah 29:11 NIV).

Today as I spent some quiet time with the Lord, I saw myself on the Potter's wheel being whirled around endlessly, so it seemed. There were many times when I became dizzy as the Great Potter was lovingly and diligently working on me. I initially found myself resenting His touch because I knew it would mean pain and suffering. So often I thought, "Lord, I'm fine right where I am;" But, He just kept right on whirling me around until He was satisfied that His work of art was to His pleasure. Eventually I was able to surrender gratitude to God for not leaving me where I was because I knew He would continue this process until He had created another High-Definition masterpiece, much greater than the previous ones. As I thought of the Potter's wheel, I envisioned several spiritual "Busts" of me all laid out in a row, each one more precious than the ones before it. They all had a special story to tell, but the greatest revelation was that my God would never leave me where I was. He never was completely satisfied with each piece because He knew that with every new whirl and touch, His work could be more fully perfected—more highly defined. I then thought: "Down through the years, we observe the different seasons of our life through our various photos. They each show how dramatically we have changed: Thinning hair; Facial changes; pain and disappointment in our eyes; illness and even weight gain." But the beauty of all of this is that while my photos may indicate the decline of my physical body, each of the Master Potter's "Busts" of me is an indication of His continuous perfecting of my inner man, all made possible because He is never willing to leave me where I am.

Prayer: Lord, how grateful I am that you never listen to me when I cry out, "That's enough!" You have the plan, and you are the only one who knows how to perfect that plan to your glory. I thank you for showing me your continuous High-Definition work in my life. It really is true that "Father knows best!" Praise the name of Jesus. Amen.

Encouragement Tip: The next time you take out those old photos and long for how you once were, remember to reflect on your spiritual snapshots and the many ways God has been perfecting you. Then decide which one has the greater importance.

Thought: Although I may not yet be all that I should be in Christ, I thank God that I am not what I once was since He began whirling me around.

Just Because I Am the Way I Am Doesn't Mean I Have to Stay This Way!

"Do not conform any longer to the pattern of this world, but be transformed by the renewing of your mind. Then you will be able to test and prove what God's will is—His good, pleasing and perfect will"

(Romans 12:2 NIV).

For many years I believed that the way I was, (my habits, idiosyncrasies, and lifestyle), was the way I would always be. I was always a type A kind of woman, with several irons in the fire—and all at the same time. I wore a hairstyle that was quick and easy, allowing me to come home from work, jump in the shower, and be off to an evening event. I was involved in a number of ministries both in and out of my home and was both a "Night Hawk" and an "Early Bird." I could get by on 3-4 hours of sleep per night, and yet keep every ball well juggled in the air. All during these years, my mother would plead for me to slow down and take better care of myself, to whom I repeatedly responded: "Live and let live. Let me be who God made me to be." I argued that you cannot change what you are. But recently, God stepped right inside of my argument and spoke words that really surprised me. I decided to take another look at Psalm 139:13 where it states that I was "knit in my mother's womb." I knew this referred to how God uniquely made me—from my personality right down to the tiniest detail of my physical make-up. I thought once a type A, always a type A but God began to make it clear that I was not allowing Him the room to transform me. My actions could only change if I would be willing to yield my thinking to Him. When it comes to God's children, except for salvation, nothing is set in stone.

Oftentimes in marriage, one spouse may say to the other: "This is the way God made me, so you must accept me just the way I am." But my question is: "Is this how God wants you to stay? It is so easy to explain away who we are by quoting Psalm 139: 13 but what does God say about it? Doesn't He want us to be pliable enough that even our personalities lay bare before Him so that He can transform us into His likeness?

Recently, my son took out some play doh that, although it was new, having been stored for a while, became brittle and difficult to work with. He began to moisten the play doh with water and knead it to make it pliable enough so that his son could fashion it to his pleasure. What a beautiful picture of how we must become in the hands of our Master Potter!

I now realize that although I am a type A personality, I must allow the Lord to change me and that just may mean slowing down my pace, getting more rest, and taking some of the irons out of the fire. It may just mean that in a marriage, although individual personalities are retained, God may need to adjust those same personalities He knitted in the womb. From God's perspective, nothing about us is set in stone; else we could never possibly bear His resemblance.

Prayer: Lord, although you gave us a starting point in the womb, it was never your intention to allow us to stay that way. During our lifetime, we become brittle and hard, requiring you to "moisten" us with your grace. Thank you for not allowing us to stay the way we are. What a testimony it is to others when they can see unmistakable evidence that our heavenly Father is busy changing His children from glory to glory! Amen.

An Angel in Stone

"I thank Christ Jesus our Lord, who has given me strength, that He considered me faithful, appointing me to His service. Even though I was once a blasphemer and a persecutor and a violent man, I was shown mercy because I acted in ignorance and unbelief. The grace of God was poured out on me abundantly along with the faith and love that are in Christ Jesus"

(1 Timothy 1:12-14 NIV).

I recall reading somewhere that Michelangelo often saw his finished works before he sculpted them. On one occasion, he was seen rolling a large, ordinary stone down the street and when asked what he would do with it, he replied, "I see an angel trying to get out."

Having been a public-school teacher for 29 years, God had given me the privilege of seeing many "Angels in stone trying to get out." I recall hosts of special education and behaviorally challenged students being transformed in my classroom, as I was able to see beyond their obvious limitations. Many of the classroom activities I planned served to bring out the best in these students, to the amazement of my colleagues and administrators.

In that same line of thinking, I praise God for seeing beyond my sinful limitations and choosing to work in my life both to will and to do of His good pleasure. I thank Him for His wonderful grace gift that did not deter Him from creating me, knowing my sinful capabilities. What a great and merciful God we have who could take a blasphemer, a persecutor, and a violent man like Paul, and transform him into the one chosen to take the gospel to the gentiles the world over. Glory to God for the great Sculptor, the great Visionary He is. What about you? Is there someone whom you can encourage to become what God created them to be? Look around you! There are lots of "Angels in stone" who are waiting for you to help them get out.

Prayer: Dear Lord, I cannot know how you could have ever seen an "Angel trying to get out of me," but I simply praise you. It amazes me that when you were creating mankind, knowing what would be in our hearts did not prevent you from giving up on us. I thank you that your transforming power will continue to perfect us until the day of Christ Jesus. May our lives bring pleasure and glory to you, our great Visionary. In Jesus' name, Amen.

"Kneed-ful"

"Therefore, my dear friends, as you have always obeyed, not only in my presence, but now much more in my absence, continue to work out your own salvation with

fear and trembling, for it is God who works in you to will and to act according to His good purpose"

(Philippians 2:12-13 NIV).

During the fall of 2004, I found myself under the scalpel as I underwent another knee replacement on the very same knee. As always, the surgery was just the beginning of a long and tedious process of recovery. One day while in therapy, I asked the therapist why the doctor could not set my knee at the required number of degrees during my surgery. This would have made my rehabilitation time span much shorter and a lot less work and pain. She stated that during the surgery, the doctor had already tested my knee to be sure that it could extend and bend to that of a normal knee. However, it was "kneed-ful" for me to work out what the doctor worked in during surgery. In other words, my doctor knew what my knee could do, but it was my responsibility to get it permanently to that place.

And so, it is with our salvation. It is a long and trying process that never gives way to a short cut. God, in His infinite wisdom, has already set in motion His plan for us. Before the foundations of the world, He knew that He would be performing my "heart" surgery and He already had an unobstructed vision of what my life in Him would become. However, it is my responsibility to cooperate with my heavenly Therapist so that I can become all that He already knows I can be in Him. There are no short cuts with God. And this is always a hard pill to swallow because we are spoiled rotten by all the sophisticated technology we have today. Although our daily lives are made easier, God still chooses the hard ways---ways that take time and require patience and perseverance. Salvation is a continuous process and although the goal has been set, I must endure so that I can reach it.

Prayer: Heavenly Father, thank you for growing us up in our salvation through your ongoing "Boot Camp" training. Although it would be easier if you would completely grow us up at the time of salvation, we thank you that salvation is a life-long process, and we must cooperate with you to reach maturity. How grateful I am when I think about how your way of doing things is so much different from the world. Thank you for making me do my part even though you already worked it in me.

"Whatever Your Lot... Clear It Off and Build Something on It!"

"Lord, you have assigned me my portion and cup; you have made my lot secure"

(Psalm 16:5 NIV).

Shortly after the construction of our house was completed, I decided to try my hand at gardening and landscaping. Where would I begin with such a monumental task? By the looks of the crabgrass and weeds, I knew I would have a real job on my hands, so I began by renting a tiller. As the tiller turned over the soil, many hidden "treasures" were revealed: rocks, glass, nails, and pieces of mortar, clay, former tree roots, and much more. After working hard to clear my future flowerbed, I watched it develop into a lovely part of the lot.

God carefully plans out our lives and His plans are established way before the foundations of the world. When He assigns us our lot, He lovingly places on it His "hidden treasures." Perhaps He will sprinkle glass into the soil to cut our heart; nails and tacks to prick our soul; just enough topsoil to enrich our lives; sandpaper to smooth out our rough edges; clay to keep us from becoming spiritual sluggards as we work our lot; and rain to promote spiritual growth. Our mission is to clear it off and build something eternal on it.

Since God is our LandLord, it is essential that we stay close to Him so we can consult Him when our lot needs to be maintained. However, no matter how hard we work to get our lot up and running, it will require the power of God to make it into something beautiful and lovely…. something to which others will be drawn. And so, it is with our lives. What will you do with the lot God has assigned you? Will you look at it with resentment, saying: "What am I supposed to do with this mess?" Will you call on the LandLord and ask Him to help you creatively work out the lot He has planned for you?

Barren and rugged lots can be very discouraging, but what excitement we feel when we can see the Master Landscaper/ Horticulturist working it into something more beautiful than our mind could ever conceive. So, saints---this is your mission, should you choose to accept it: "Whatever your lot may be, clear it off and build something on it.

Prayer: Lord, you are the Master Landscaper of the lots you assign us. Help us, when we are tempted to compare, complain, lose heart about our lots, and try to fix them ourselves. Teach us to graciously accept each lot you assign us and with your help, make it into an unimaginable place of beauty. Amen.

Encouragement Tip: Consider the special lot God has handed to you at this time in your life. What will you do with it to bring glory to His name? Spend some quiet time reflecting on your lot and seek God's will in how you will clear it off and build something lovely on it. You'd be surprised at how creative you can become once you decide to look for God in the mix.

"Hoagie Rolls and Jesus"

"I am the Vine; you are the branches. If a man remains in me and I in him, he will bear much fruit; apart from me you can do nothing"

(John 15:5 NIV).

Hoagies bring back special memories of my growing-up years in Pennsylvania. My siblings and I loved hoagies so much that we could hardly wait to receive our allowance so we could buy one. Recently, I began to think about what it is that makes these hoagies so special. Without the unique Italian roll, the hoagie would be nothing! The roll is the reason this sandwich stands far above all other sandwiches in its category.

In John 15:5, Jesus tells us that by ourselves, we can do nothing. We become ineffective and unproductive when we separate ourselves from our Vine. Jesus is the Hoagie roll and we are the filling. He makes us look and taste good! Without Him, we are just like those ordinary sandwiches that taste like all the others.

It would be as if we had made a hoagie without the Italian roll. Now that's just plain unimaginable!

In like manner, it is unimaginable for me to live my life without being connected to Jesus. There would be no Holy Spirit power to strengthen me that I might have great endurance and patience. My life would be as ordinary, plain, and dull as those who walk apart from Christ. There would be nothing attractive about my soul that would draw others to what I have in the Lord.

Wherever I have lived in America, I have never been able to find the likes of the Pennsylvania hoagie because the authentic Italian roll is unique to the Delaware Valley area. Its goodness is indescribable to one who never had one. Likewise, Jesus is indescribable. If you never experienced Him, there is no way to understand who He is. This is a case of Jesus being the best thing that ever happened to me!

Prayer: Lord, thank you for the delicious hoagie, but more importantly, thank you for the spiritual analogy of the Italian hoagie roll you have given me. You are the best thing that ever happened to me, and I thank you that throughout the universe, there is no one like you. You stand in a class all by yourself. Amen.

Encouragement tip: Knowing Christ and putting yourself down is an oxymoron. If the Italian hoagie roll is the thing that makes the hoagie stand out, how much more will the Christ in you make you a shining star? Remember this formula: Christ + you=something wonderful!

Can You Find *Jesus* in Your Picture?

"You will seek me and find me when you seek me with all your heart. Then I will be found by you"

(Jeremiah 29:13-14a NIV).

As a child, I really loved the puzzles in which you were to find a given object: "Can you find all the monkeys in this picture?" It would be so much fun looking for each monkey, but oftentimes, just when I thought I'd found them all, I would eventually see one or two more that I had initially overlooked. I found it interesting how the artist could cleverly camouflage the monkeys in the total setting. There would be monkeys in places that you would never expect to find. Eventually, when I thought I was finished locating each monkey, I was surprised to see that there were so many more remaining than I could imagine. The kicker is this: They were there all the time. However, my question for those who know the Lord is: "Can you find Jesus in your picture?"

During the past two years, the Lord has been teaching me to see Him in the everyday mix of things. It is so difficult to see Him anywhere when the pressures of life come closing in on us. Jesus is camouflaged when things are deteriorating. We begin to ask ourselves, "Where could God be in all of this?" God has been wonderfully revealing to me that He is always in my picture— good, bad, or ugly. The first thing I have learned to do is to *run* to Him and quietly sit at His feet. It is when I begin the diligent search to find Him in my picture that, just as with the hidden monkeys, I will eventually see Him. An interesting example of this is found in this season of menopause I am facing. It is terribly uncomfortable with the hot flashes and sweats. I must keep a towel in my purse and in every room of my house. However, I recently learned that hot flashes serve as a type of de-toxin. Because of their intense heat, the body goes through an intense cleansing. I can now see Jesus in my picture because He has made it possible for something good to come out of something as horrible as hot flashes.

It is my prayer that you, too will decide to seek God with all your heart so that you can always find Him in your picture.

Prayer: Lord, You and You only are the awesome God. Everything you do is good whether we like it or not. I thank you that you have instructed us to diligently seek you and have also promised us rewards when we do so. It is so comforting to know that even when you are camouflaged in the big picture, you still can be found. Daily show us how to find you and give you the praise you so deserve. Amen.

Encouragement Tip: Get serious about being at Jesus' feet and learn of Him. He will teach you the deep things about your sufferings and struggles, and then His presence will become visible to your soul's eye. Remember: He is there all along!

Restored to Bring Glory

"And the God of all grace, who called you to His eternal glory in Christ, after you have suffered a little while, will Himself restore you, and make you strong, firm, and steadfast"

(1 Peter 5:10 NIV).

After a season of beautiful productivity, I noticed that my rose knockouts were beginning to droop and had suddenly lost their fruit-bearing potential. I initially suspected the intense heat to be the culprit, but after a closer look, I realized that my roses were suffering from a severe beetle attack. Numerous Japanese beetles were heavily weighing down the bushes as they declared an unmerciful war on their foliage. Now, having made a substantial investment in the landscaping of my yard, I absolutely refused to take this attack lying down. I immediately contacted an insecticide company to begin treatment on my rose bushes. About 3 hours after having been sprayed, I witnessed a miracle as I backed out of my garage. Two bushes had become fruitful again as they burst forth with brand new roses. I could not believe my eyes! It was so dramatic and yet, quite beautiful!

Sometimes our lives are just like those rose bushes. They are weighed down with the "beetles" of worldly cares: anxiety, worry, disappointment, confusion, and hopelessness. We have even experienced seasons when we suffer so many different attacks simultaneously, that just like those rose bushes, we cannot bloom as God intends. So, what can we do to put those "beetles" out of business? We need a squirt of Holy Spirit Power to be applied to our souls. This can only happen when we abide in Christ, allowing His power to rest on us. Spending quiet times at His feet along with memorizing and claiming His word, can assist us in standing firm in our faith. In doing so, our heavenly Father restores us so that we can bring Him the glory He so well deserves. So, Saints, get rid of those "beetles" and allow your spiritual fruit to come bursting forth with beauty and grace!

Prayer: Father, just as all creation glorifies you by being free to do what you created it to do, may we also be free from the "beetles" of our lives so that we can glorify you. Spray us with your Holy Spirit Power and make us bug-free. Amen.

Isn't It Reassuring?

Being confident of this, that he who began a good work in you will carry it on to completion until the day of Christ Jesus'

(Philippians 1:6 NIV).

Spring is by far, the most amazing season of all! Suddenly buds appear from nowhere and the landscape is wonderfully rejuvenated! It is as though the barren land has awakened from a long, deep sleep and everything is starting to grow again! I find it hard to imagine that, despite the winter's frigid temperatures and the numerous snowstorms, death is preparing to give birth to such beauty.

I remember taking walks on the snow and ice-covered streets of my neighborhood and thinking about how difficult it is to foresee the beauty of spring, especially after such a long and hard winter. But eventually, just like clockwork, the winter passes away and wonderfully the buds begin to appear.

Sometimes we struggle with the assurance of our salvation in that same way. We enter a season of barrenness—a dry spell in our spiritual life. We become distracted by the things of the world and appear to have little desire to be enclosed with God. We say things or do things that Satan uses against us by whispering discouraging comments in our ears: "And you call yourself a Christian? A real Christian could never do such things!" Just as the hopelessness of winter sets in and there seems to be no signs of life, our hearts are left in a state of deep despair all because the enemy of our soul has successfully set us up with another one of his clever smokescreens. The result is that we begin to buy into his lies and to doubt our salvation. What then must we do? We must return to the starting point of our salvation and remember the precious promises of God. It is necessary to recall our position in Christ and who we are in Him. We must remember that He who started such great salvation in us, will always stand in His commitment to keep it going, even when we experience those dormant seasons in our spiritual life.

As I began writing these website devotionals, the enemy began to remind me of the spiritually dormant seasons I had been going through last year. He incessantly taunted me with thoughts of inadequacy and had even attacked my security in the sufficiency of Christ. But the Holy Spirit's voice quietly reminded me that, just as under the winter's snow a beautiful flower is preparing to burst forth, so it is with me. It is in the inactivity of the cold season that God is up to something great! I praise the Lord that not one of His precious promises has fallen to the ground. May we stay strong in Him who always completes His work in us.

Prayer: Dear Lord, oh how I thank you for all your precious promises. It gives me great encouragement to know that unlike us, you are a God of your word. May we walk in our salvation in the same way we received you---and that is by faith. Please help us to keep our hearts on things above where you are seated at the right hand of God. For it is when we remember where you are, that we can know our position in you and be certain that our salvation is a done deal! In Jesus' name, amen

Look at Your Master!

"Since then, you have been raised with Christ, set your hearts on things above where Christ is seated at the right hand of God. Set your minds on things above, not on earthly things for you died and your life is now hidden with Christ in God. When Christ who is your life appears, then you will also appear with Him in glory"

(Colossians 3:1-4 NIV).

I am amazed at dogs and what they can be taught to do. They are so much more trainable than humans! I am told that dogs experience a very rigorous course of training while in obedience school. Some of their training involves being taught to look at their master. When the dog can successfully do this at command, he is then taken to a higher degree of training when a nice juicy steak is placed in front of him. At this point, the dog has forgotten to look at his master because the competing steak distracts him. Upon gazing at the steak, the dog is repeatedly reminded to look at his master, and after some serious whimpering, he will inevitably go for the steak. However, each time the dog sets his heart on the steak, he must start all over again. Eventually his whimpering becomes shorter and less intense until he can finally look at his master and treat the steak as a secondary interest.

This dog training is a beautiful illustration of what Paul is saying in Colossians 3:1-4. We are instructed to "Look at our Master," but Satan is always waiting to dangle before us the "juicy steaks" of lust, the cares of life, materialism, busyness, slothfulness, entertainment, toys, and careers. I often hear Christians lamenting over their tendency to clutter their days with everything else except abiding in Jesus. They fail to study the word to show themselves approved, and Bible memorization is "impossible" because the cares of the world keep them going all day. We often forget that we have died to ourselves and are now hidden with Christ in God. In other words, we no longer engineer our own lives, but look at our Master and allow Him to be Executor and Lord. Matthew 6:21 states, "For where your treasure is, there your heart will be also." Could it be that our hearts are really on the "steak" and not on our Master? Let us pray that our God will work in us both the desire and the ability to put Him first if He is first, He can not only give us His bigger and juicier "steaks," but also, so much more!

Prayer: Dear Lord, for the present time we find such attraction to the earthly things that surround us every day. Help us to reject the wrong things and begin storing up for our eternity with you. Teach us to always look at you for nothing in this world can ever compare with you. May we always cherish the Master more than the meat. Amen.

Worship Lessons from The Magi

"On coming to the house, they saw the Child with his mother Mary, and they bowedand worshiped him. Then they opened their treasures and presented him with gifts of gold and incense and of myrrh"

(Matthew 2:11 NIV).

I have recently been studying the Christmas story, particularly the segment regarding the Magi's search for the Christ Child. There is so much that inspires me about this account.

Although these wise men were gentile kings, somehow, they had learned about the prophecy that Jesus would be born the King of the Jews. In other words, they had done their homework and followed it up with a diligent and fervent search for this major event. I understand that their pilgrimage to Jerusalem took several years. It would have been very tempting for them to turn back because of the time span, and the challenging terrains and weather conditions that lay ahead. Yet, they moved as men who were on a mission. And just what was this mission? Their solitary purpose was to worship the baby Jesus. I wonder if they faced ridicule as they inquired where this baby could be found? Whatever their situation, they were in it for the long-haul—not shrinking back and refusing to return to the east having failed to complete this mission. When they finally did reach the manger in which Jesus was born, they were able to consummate their search by first, giving themselves to Him, and then presenting Him with their precious material treasures.

I decided to do a study on the word, "worship" as used in Matthew 2:11 and I found that it means to kiss---like a dog licking his master's hand. I thought it interesting that a dog would be the analogy used here. Dogs are loyal to their masters; they love them unconditionally and usually follow them wherever they go.

What about us? Oftentimes our loyalty is reserved for the seeking of that special gift for our spouses, children, or grandchildren. We diligently seek out the malls, catalogs, or go wherever and pay whatever we need to make someone happy at Christmas. Oh, how wonderful it would be if we would seek Jesus with such diligence and tenacity! The Christmas season would take on a whole new meaning if we were willing to make it the starting point of going all out—ridicule or not—to worship the One who went all out for us.

The Magi were on to something big because although they were not Jewish, they are continuing to teach Christians today how we must seek God with all our heart. They teach us lessons about dying to self and making every effort to lay aside all things that would get in the way of our worshiping the one true God. Have you done your homework as you annually prepare for Christmas? If so, will you prepare for this magnificent event with the same fervency and diligence of the Magi? During each Christmas season, will your sole purpose be to worship Jesus with that same kind of priority? It is my prayer that in all your future Christmas preparations and celebrations that Christ will be at the very center of your life and worship.

Prayer: Lord, thank you that even in our times, we can still learn worship lessons from the Magi. Help us to desire that same kind of diligence and fervor as we worship you at Christmas. May this great lesson be but the beginning of our "licking your hand," not only at Christmas, but also the other 364 days of the year. Amen.

Bloom Like its Still Summer!

"Preach the word; be prepared in season and out of season"

(2 Timothy 4:2 NIV).

As I rolled up my blinds, I noticed how incredibly beautiful my dahlias were. They were budding and blooming in all their glory, as they seemed to shout: *"We're not finished yet!"* Now you might say, "No big deal, that's what dahlias should be doing." But did I tell you that it was the middle of November and that they were blooming like it was still summer? Despite the low overnight temperatures and even some consistently light frost, they were determined to continue doing what they were created to do, and to do it until the very end! In fact, just a few days before the life-threatening frost set in, I was able to collect a beautiful bouquet of dahlias, enough to fill a large vase.

As I took a final glimpse of these beautiful flowers that adorned my lawn so late in the season, I was reminded of my own spiritual life. Psalm 92:14 states that the righteous will continue to bear fruit in old age and will stay fresh and green. If you couple this scripture with Colossians 3:23, "Whatever you do, work at it with all your heart for the Lord," you have a Biblical description of what my dahlias were doing. They knew not that it was the middle of November, or that at any time, their beautiful life span would be over. They knew only one thing and that was that they would bloom with all their might to please their Creator!

I want to serve the Lord with fervor! In these last days I do not want to become faint, to quit, or to become so pre-occupied with what season it is that I cease to bear fruit. I want to live for the Lord in and out of season so that I will be doing just what He created me to do, and that is to "Bloom Like It's Still Summer!"

Prayer: Lord, I can often find you in my spiritual picture, and the beautiful dahlias you have given me are just another way to see you. Thank you for the lovely inspirational message they spoke to me when I noticed they were still there blooming with all their might. I pray that this special reminder will encourage me to never retire from the calling you have placed on my life. In fact, let me make it a daily goal to "Bloom Like It's Still Summer!" Amen.

From Disappointment to His-Appointment

"But God sent me ahead of you to preserve for you a remnant on earth to save your lives by a great deliverance"

(Genesis 45:7 NIV).

Joseph has always been one of my favorite and well-respected Bible characters. His willingness and ability to play the hand he was dealt has impressed me. Except for one recorded incident, the Bible does not portray him as one who complained about his many misfortunes. In fact, Joseph was quite gifted in making the best lemonade from the bitterest lemons. Having humbled himself under the mighty hand of God, he was eventually exalted to second in command under Pharaoh.

Life has its way of moving in directions that we could never expect. Like Joseph, we find ourselves in situations that seem unfair. I remember feeling this way when I was left to raise my two sons alone. Although it was not my desire to do so, God saw fit to *bless* me with this ministry.

Today, many grandparents are facing a second round of parenting as they struggle to raise their grandchildren. Insecure and ill-prepared adult children are throwing the parenting baton to the ground, leaving their parents with the huge responsibility of rearing their children. This certainly is not what grandparents have expected. At the very season they should be planning cruises, instead, they are hanging out at the playground.

How should grandparents respond to such unfairness? Many are bitter because both their golden years and finances are being absorbed raising a second family. However, I believe that like Joseph, grandparents can be wonderfully used to touch the future through these challenging circumstances. In other words, God can take them from disappointment to His-appointment.

Psalm 139:16 reminds us that all the days of our lives were recorded in God's book before any of them came to be. This indicates that God had already planned for and preserved a generation of grandparents to pick up the baton and raise their grandchildren.

I have found that there may be several benefits that can be derived from this "parenting-again" role, such as: having a greater purpose for living; having the chance to raise the grandchild differently than they did their own adult children; receiving love and companionship from grandchildren; re-connecting generations that have been broken; continuing family histories, and feeling younger because the grandchildren are present in the home.

Just as Joseph was sent ahead to preserve a remnant for God's purposes, some grandparents are called by God to accomplish this very same thing. But usually when we hear about grandparents having to raise their grandchildren, we tend to sigh and say, "That's a shame!" But is it? In God's great mercy, He is raising up grandparents to pass down to their grandchildren the memorial stones of God's faithfulness. I cannot think of any greater ministry for God's kingdom than grandparents who are called to live out their golden years impacting their grandchildren's lives for Christ's sake. So, if you are a grandparent who feels "stuck" raising your grandchildren, rejoice that God has entrusted you with so great a ministry. I am grateful for all the grandparents who have entered this role. In fact, at this writing, I am personally joining the ranks of grandparents who are picking up dropped batons in preparation for the next generation. I echo Paul's words in 1 Timothy 1:12: "I thank Christ Jesus our Lord who gives me strength, that He considered me faithful, appointing me to His service." And part of that service includes raising my three grandchildren.

Prayer: Dear God, as you appoint grandparents to raise or provide day care for their grandchildren, please grant them the grace, patience, and faithfulness necessary to accomplish this important calling. Teach them to embrace this calling with a positive attitude. May they cherish this opportunity to impact the next generation for the kingdom of God---a generation that could otherwise be lost. Impress upon the church the need to walk beside these grandparents in support of this difficult calling. May we ever encourage them to persevere as they press toward the mark of the high calling of God in Christ Jesus. Amen.

Whistle While You Wait

"I have learned the secret of being content in any and every situation, whether well fed or hungry, whether living in plenty or in want. I can do everything through Christ who gives me strength"

(Philippians 4:12-13 NIV).

"I guess people see me as a freak or something. All my friends are married, and I cannot even get a date! What's wrong with me?" These words, having been expressed by a single young woman, cut deeply into my heart. Although I do not personally know what it is like to be thirty-something and un-married, I do know of the anguish expressed by so many dissatisfied singles. However, when I study the Bible, I am encouraged by what I have found. God addresses discontent in several places in the scriptures, and although they are general in nature, they can most definitely be applied to the "being single" dilemma.

In Jeremiah 29:4-9, the Lord sent a message to His people who had been exiled to Babylon. He knew of their despair and discontent in this foreign place, but He commanded them to go on with their lives. They were instructed to build houses, marry, plant gardens, and pray for the place of their captivity. In other words, God wanted them to take their undesirable circumstances and live them out to His glory.

In Philippians 2:14, we are commanded to "Do all things without murmuring or complaining so that we may become blameless and pure children of God without fault in a crooked and depraved generation." God has called us all to some specific purpose in our lives on earth. Being single may be one such calling and when singles refuse to be content, they sin. Being content is a learned behavior and has nothing to do with what is going right or wrong in your life. It means trusting God even when your circumstances are undesirable. It means making the choice to fervently serve God in singleness and to be careful not to fill your life up with substitutes---anything that will help you escape the reality of your singleness. Decide to practice contentment daily and leave your singleness to the One who has called you to it. While you wait for your breakthrough---contentment with or without a spouse---be deliberate about faithfully and diligently doing God's work. Whistle while you wait!

Prayer: Heavenly Father, you have called some of your children to be single and satisfied. In their own strength, they could never attain such a goal. As you did with Paul, please teach them and all your saints to be contented whatever the circumstances and to walk with confidence in the calling you have given them. Help the church to embrace them as vibrant members of the whole body of Christ. Amen.

Seasonal Beauty

In everything give thanks: For this is the will of God in Christ Jesus concerning you

(1 Thessalonians 5:18 NIV).

Although I usually try to have a thankful heart in all circumstances, it seems that this year I have found something quite unique for which I am learning to be thankful. Recently, the Sovereign Lord has caused me to reflect on the aging process and to appreciate it for the thing of beauty that it is.

"The Lord does not look at the things man looks at. Man looks at the outward appearance, but the Lord looks at the heart"

(1 Samuel 16:7 NIV).

This past September, I traveled to Oklahoma to see three dear friends whom I had not seen for nearly twenty years. I must confess that I initially felt a little nervous about seeing them because I was not exactly the way they last remembered me to be. So much had happened to my physical and emotional being. A stroke, seven knee surgeries, the effects of menopause, raising grandchildren, disappointments, heartaches, and thyroid disease had all taken their toll on my outward man. What would my friends think about how I had changed and how important would that be to them, or even to me? However, when my first two friends and I were reunited, everything went well as we hugged one another's necks. Outwardly we had all changed, but that was expected because we had all moved to a different season of our lives during this twenty-year period.

"She is clothed with strength and dignity; she can laugh at the days to come"

(Proverbs 31:25 NIV).

When I visited the third friend, an interesting but thought-provoking thing occurred. She greeted me with, "You put on all that weight, but your face is still pretty." Now normally, a comment like that would make this sister's jaws tight. But wonderfully, the Holy Spirit kicked in when He reminded me about the good changes in my Spirit-man. This friend proceeded to share with me that she was having some major crises in her life and had no idea as to how she should handle them. But didn't I remember she had been ordained to preach a few years ago?

Anyway, as I pulled out of her driveway, I yelled to her, "Read 2 Chronicles 20 and Isaiah 41:10." I had hardly gotten to the main road when she rang me on my cell and ecstatically thanked me for the scriptures and proclaimed that God had sent me to Oklahoma on a mission. Ta, Ta! Just then, a Holy Spirit light bulb went off in my head: "Is it more important to look the same way I looked twenty years ago and yet have nothing spiritual to offer or to have endured physical changes while becoming rich in the things of the Lord?" With every physical and emotional trial, I had experienced, a spiritual lesson had been gained and growth had occurred. God had enabled the spirit-man of my heart to have something spiritually substantial to offer someone who had a desperate need. My dress size could never touch that.

"Charm is deceptive, and beauty is fleeting, but a woman who fears the Lord is to be praised'

(Proverbs 31:30 NIV).

"He grew up be fore Him like a tender shoot and like a root out of dry ground. He had no beauty or majesty to attract us to Him, nothing in His appearance that we should desire Him"

(Isaiah 53:2NIV).

And so it is that I have yet a new reason to thank God at Thanksgiving. There is a seasonal beauty that we sometimes overlook. Just as there is beauty in the spring when the buds appear and wonderfully rejuvenate the landscape, and in the summer, these same buds give way to the newness of life in all its glory, and where autumn struts its stuff as it shouts out its last hurrah before death sets in, so it is with the seasonal beauty of our lives. And even in winter, the season of death, ice covered trees and snowy landscapes are beautiful scenes painted by the hands of God Almighty! There is no season without beauty and so it is with our appointed time on this earth, especially when our spirit-man is always being renewed from day to day.

Thought: Where do you place your beauty, today? Cosmetics, make-up, beauty aids and holistic diets are great, but Holy Spirit beauty surpasses them all and lasts through all the seasons of life. May we look like our Heavenly Father everyday!

Prayer: My Father, you do all things well and at their proper time. Although we may not always feel good about the outward changes in our bodies, I thank you that you want us to know that our inward man is being renewed daily and that is what you desire for us. May we get in the habit of accentuating what is more important. Teach us to become spiritually enriched so we can make a difference in the lives of those we encounter in our daily lives. Amen.

"The end of a matter is better than its beginning"

(Ecclesiastes 7:8a NIV).

Afterword

As mentioned earlier in this book, John 10:10 has greatly impacted my life. Jesus encourages us by telling us that He came to give us abundant life. I would like to leave you with a poem that describes this abundant life and I pray that you will diligently seek it as you live out each day.

Higher Grounds

It was just a few short years ago when I suddenly realized

That God was quietly rearranging the seasons of my life.

It was He who placed this longing in my heart to ask: "What now?

What new calling do you have for me, and will you show me how?"

In answering these questions, God was prompting me to see,

The variety of spiritual gifts He had lovingly poured into me.

As I began to examine each gift, my mind came to reason

That teaching was still my calling in this life's brand-new season.

Having spent more than half of my years in public education,

I thought perhaps this teaching thing had reached its cessation.

Then God began to stir my soul, saying: "I have much for you to do.

Dare to leave your comfort zone and let me work through you.

Mediocrity and status quo are no longer the order of the day.

'Cause in this brand-new season of life, Higher Grounds is the only way."

Now all this conversing with the Lord about His Higher Grounds,

Convinced me that without it, the Abundant Life could not be found.

I asked the Lord, "What does this thing called Abundant Life look like?"

He said, "It's being strengthened with all power according to my glorious might.

It's about my strength made perfect in your weakness everyday,

And seeing beyond your circumstances when smokescreens get in the way.

It's about sitting in the back seat and leaving the driving to me,

While trusting me with every traffic jam and pothole you will see.

It's about emerging from the 'rides of life' with a legacy to share

With the next generation who will one day be right there.

So, don't throw away your confidence or faint along the way,

Since I expect to find great faith when I return one day."

As my conversation with God was concluded, it became quite clear to me:

Although promotions come with a high price tag, Higher Grounds is the best place to be.

God be with you.

Deborah R. Reaves

Subject Index

God's Plan---From Disappointment to His Appointment

God's provision----Right Under My Nose

Godliness----Soul Visions

Grace---Spandex Grace/ Flood Proof Toilets

Image of God----High-Definition Pottery

Imitating Christ---Invisible Tattoos

Intimacy---Breast Feeding

Joint Heirs---Benefits

Obedience----From Water to Wine

Patience and Endurance----What God Taught Me in the Torture Chamber/ Bloom Like it's Still Summer

Perseverance---Weed Lessons/ Working with A Sword Handy

Seeking Jesus---Can You Find Jesus in this Picture?

Spiritual Maturity----Seeing in Spiritual 3-D

Submission---Dead Men Can't Talk

The Tongue----Mouth-to-Mouth Resuscitation

Transformation---Defeated Doesn't Live Here Anymore/ An Angel in Stone/Just Because I am the Way I am

Working out Salvation---Kneed-ful/whatever Your Lot

Worship---Worship Lessons from the Magi